YOUNG MUSLIMS SPEAK

Copies of this report are available at:
www.peacedirect.org

ISBN
978-0-9552419-0-1
0-9552419-0-1

Cover photographs by: Richard Mallinson
Back cover: report participants photographed by Kois Miah at
19 Princelet Street - Britain's Museum of Immigration and Diversity.
Cover design by: Iain Lanyon www.keanlanyon.com
Illustrations and typesetting by: Iain Lanyon
Printed and bound by: Print Solutions www.printsolutionsuk.com

Young Muslims Speak is published by
Peace Direct
Development House
56-64 Leonard Street
London EC2A 4JX
www.peacedirect.org

About Peace Direct

Peace Direct works with grassroots peacebuilders both within the United Kingdom and abroad to alleviate conflict at all levels of society. As part of our work, we use the experience gained in one conflict and look at ways in which this knowledge can be put to good use in preventing others. Knowledge sharing not only helps us to better tackle conflict but, by comparison, furthers our knowledge of the root causes of conflict.

www.peacedirect.org

Acknowledgements

The Young Muslims Speak project would not have been possible without the energy, determination and commitment of all those involved. If it has been a transforming experience for some, it is certainly due to the honesty, passion and desire for change of all participants, whether at the workshops, in the dialogue session, follow ups or just as commentators. A special thank you must go to Dekha Ibrahim Abdi and Mohammed Shybta, whose thought-provoking interventions sparked stimulating conversations. Hilde Rapp was invaluable in holding these conversations with great gentleness and in offering her knowledge and networking skills. The project team, Jonathan Hill, Abul Kalam and Sophie Millner, has proved indefatigable in supporting the process and organising the events. We would like to thank the contributors to this publication who have juggled their commitments to meet our deadlines. Last but not least we are grateful for the help and consideration of the following; Ruth Musgrave who advised us wisely, Iain Lanyon who accommodated all our needs, and Francesca Cerletti who oversaw the project from start to finish.

Peace Direct

How did it all start?

9/11 has been described as a turning point for many across the globe. In the UK the attack on the World Trade Centre lead to the affirmation of broad brushed references to Islam and Muslims in large sections of the media. It has been a crescendo culminating in talks of a clash of civilizations between Islam and the West.

Suddenly what was for many a parallel world became something to discover. Increasingly new attempts were made to understand the views of the Muslim communities in the UK. However, their perspectives have mostly been filtrated through preconceived ideas resulting in a distorted end product.

The July 2005 London bombings suddenly catapulted young British Muslims into the spotlight. They have been surrounded by discussions focussing on terrorism, radicalisation, incompatibility and conflict. During this debate the opinions and views of young Muslims have not been sought on their own terms and have been overshadowed by misconceptions and the need to create a 'story'.

Has anybody given a voice and listened to young Muslims' own views on these issues? What is really going on in their communities? What is actually important to them? What are their needs? Which ways forward do they see? Could tools developed in other countries where communal tension exists be used to bring a fresh perspective to the UK context? These were questions Peace Direct set out to explore, using Muslims facilitators from Kenya and Palestine to stimulate discussion with groups of young Muslims from a wide range of cultural and ethnic backgrounds.

CONTENTS

EXECUTIVE SUMMARY

Why did we start this project? In the wake of the July 2005 London bombings young British Muslims became surrounded by discussions on terrorism, radicalisation, incompatibility and conflict. Although receiving strong media interest, they felt that where their views were sought, the resulting reports were often coloured by preconceived ideas. A real need existed for young British Muslims to be heard on their own terms. What is really going on in their communities? What is actually important to them? What are their needs? And mostly what ways forward do they see? This report is based on workshops and dialogue sessions involving in depth discussions and exploration of these issues. This report itself emphasises action; a direct reflection of the strong message expressed by the young Muslims participating in the project.

Addressing the needs of a diverse group such as young British Muslims requires stepping away from the perspective of homogeneity to seek to understand first hand what is needed. As one participant said, "*the label 'young Muslim' is very narrowing, as if that's it, there are no other layers to you as a person*". Clearly this term fails to do justice to the impressive diversity it pertains to embody. Young British Muslims know what they want and how their ideas can be achieved, but what is needed is the recognition and understanding to realise their goals.

Needs identified
Constructed through the interplay of influences from community, education, religion and family, young British Muslims feel a need to ground their **identities** in the context of their cultural heritage. **Role models and leaders** who really listen and represent the views of the young people are sorely lacking but are a potentially highly influential part of young people's lives. Young British Muslims are deeply concerned about the way they are portrayed in the **media**. "*Nobody has ever come to talk to us. You're the first person who talked to us about*

1

these things." Reaching out to those who need it most is a serious challenge but **participation and engagement** would avoid resources being wasted.

Finding solutions

Developing self-confidence and energy requires an environment within which to engage and question and from which to develop a coherent sense of identity. Role models play a critical role in motivation and guidance but young Muslims note a marked lack of connection with their elders. Education too is seen to provide a valuable opportunity to explore identity, learn about heritage and help young Muslims balance the complex mixture of influences and challenges in their lives.

Action and involvement from those working at policy, community and individual levels is needed. The development of long term relationships with local authorities is key to reaching the most disaffected and disengaged members of the community. Building relationships is as much about the quality of the communication as it is about who is engaged. Strengthening internal community relationships for example between young Muslims and community leaders are as important as building external channels of communication to society as a whole both on an individual and a collective basis.

Finding 'Community Liaison Officers' with the life experience and grassroots knowledge to act as 'true' representatives of their community and the young is one example of how to build relationships and enhance outreach work.

Receiving recognition. Muslims *"feel they have no voice"*. They want the **media** to be a friend not an enemy and are frustrated by their unfair portrayal. *"The complexities of the Muslim community are rarely accurately tackled mainly because of a lack of information."* The media should be *"more proactive and build relationships with the community and not just with 'community leaders'"*. Equally the young people have to engage with the media. Public interest needs to be more constant and proactive, rather than a reaction to external criticism. More initiatives need to continue to spread a fair and more informed understanding of Islam.

"The label itself, 'young Muslims', simplifies a community, strips it of any layers so that identity can be more easily controlled." Young British Muslims have very different life experiences, needs and abilities, and the solutions they proposed to address these needs can be understood as part of a self-reinforcing process of Engagement, Empowerment and Recognition, which holds the potential to strengthen relationships and build on the work already being done.

Young British Muslims are actively engaging in dialogue. The invitation is there to join the conversation. It's time for everyone to respond.

Sophie Millner

Unattributed quotations used in this report are comments made by participants over the course of the Young Muslims Speak project.

THE PURPOSE OF DIALOGUE

All young people grow up in an environment that offers both opportunities and challenges. Their ability to fulfil themselves depends on the balance between these forces. Young people benefit from being able to fulfil their potential but so, obviously, does society as a whole.

There are still communities in the UK that can achieve more but have yet to overcome obstacles that stand in their way. The Muslim community is one of them.

- **There are 1.6 million Muslims living in the UK today.**
- **Muslims have a long history in the UK. One of the first British Muslim communities emerged in London around 1627.**
- **The first Mosque was established in 1889 in Woking.**
- **The majority of today's Muslim families arrived in the 1950s from the former British colonies in India, including Pakistan and Bangladesh.**
  Source: BBC Religion and Ethics
  National Statistics

This is apparent in national statistics on wealth, health, crime and education; but there are also the underlying factors that are harder to measure such as self-confidence, outlook on life and sense of personal achievement, which are equally important in people's lives.

- **20% of 16-24 year old Muslims are unemployed.**
- **16% of women and 13% of men report poor health, the highest of all UK religious groups.**
- **31% of young British Muslims leave school with no qualifications compared to 15% of the total population.**
  Source: National Statistics

The increased focus recently on British Muslims has high-lighted some of the issues and feelings that young Muslims are facing within and from outside of their communities.

This report represents the ideas that emerged over a series of workshops and one-on-one dialogue sessions. Young Muslims from all over the UK pointed out the challenges they feel are most critical, and highlighted positive steps that can be taken to enable them to realise their full potential.

TODAY'S YOUNG MUSLIMS

The 1.6 million Muslims living in the UK today constitute the second largest religious group in the country. It is also the youngest with over a third of British Muslims under the age of 16. This equates to a total of over half a million young people, more than the entire population of a major British city such as Liverpool.

  * **46% of Muslims are at least second generation.**
    Source: National Statistics

Who are young Muslims? It is tempting to see young Muslims as a homogenous group. However, the term young Muslim describes a large spectrum of individuals from different ethnic and cultural backgrounds and with different nuances in their religious practices. Furthermore like other individuals identified in terms of their faith, such as 'Jews' or 'Christians', some Muslims are nominally so, but still feel a sense of political/social solidarity with their community. One young Muslim's perspective, therefore, may be completely at odds with another's as their views are formed by a mixture of aspects that make up each individual's life experience (e.g. ethnicity, education, religion, family and local culture).

"The term young Muslim is very narrowing as if that's it, there's no other layers to you as a person. It's not a title we've chosen, it's been ascribed to us."

This diversity is welcomed in Islam since its followers come from a huge variety of cultures and backgrounds. It is important to recognise the differences between them, even though Muslim communities in the UK see themselves belonging to the same family. Every young Muslim must therefore be understood as an *individual* and not only in terms of his or her faith. Diversity is an opportunity, not a barrier. Recognising individuality opens up the way to engage using diverse approaches. The individual that doesn't fit the stereotype is more the norm than the exception. Addressing the needs of such a large and diverse group is demanding, but becomes clearer through listening to those closest to the challenges and solutions, i.e. young Muslims themselves. There can be a tendency to emphasise the issues that are the easiest to deal with. However, this can lead to a distorted view in which difficult but important issues are left unchallenged. Bringing real change to communities therefore requires an open mind where those in charge of services and resources put aside their own preconceptions and ideas and seek to understand at first hand what is really needed.

Despite their differences however, young Muslims do have mutually shared overall goals. The commonly shared element among the young Muslims who participated in the project was their awareness of the situation within Muslim communities and their resourcefulness when it came to making the most of every opportunity available.

Young Muslims already know what they want to see happen in their communities and how this can be achieved. What is needed is to turn those ideas into action. This is the most important finding of the project; *young Muslims are ready and able to take greater control over their own destinies wherever they are given the opportunity.*

Ali al-Khoei - My schooling experiences as a Muslim youth

As a child I joined my local primary school and from an early age I remember a big difference between my home life and school life. I remember vividly at the age of eight when my school celebrated the Muslim festival of Eid for the first time. I remember telling my parents something extraordinary had happened, where our culture and religion had been acknowledged and how the whole school had shared the spirit of this event.

My secondary school was a Muslim one, and although I felt more at ease, I did miss all my non-Muslim friends. It is true that here I enjoyed a better community spirit, discipline, sense of security and belonging. Despite the high academic achievements of this school, I do feel more interaction is needed with other non-Muslim schools.

For my A-levels I moved to a predominantly white, state-run sixth form. I was both amused and intimidated by the negative and stereotypical notions students held towards me. I found it difficult to strike a balance between integrating, and my religion. It is not difficult to imagine why I could have easily given up and failed, but with the help of a handful of other Muslim pupils, I decided to weather the storm. With our determination to interact we were broadly accepted by the majority of pupils. As we got to reason with those who held Islamophobic views, we discovered that there is more to unite us than to divide us and we should never fall victim to stereotypes - be it our own or those of others.

ESTABLISHING NEEDS

The important issues highlighted by young Muslims are inter-linked and can be hard to disentangle since they have developed along with each other over years and sometimes carry legacies of centuries. It is possible however to broadly divide these issues into four categories that illustrate how individual issues relate to each other and form the wider context:

Identity and heritage
Who are we? It is perhaps the most difficult question for any group of people. For many young Muslims, their sense of identity is formed from a mixture of experiences within the community, educational institutions, religion and family. Sometimes, the interplay between these may cause confusion for some young Muslims. A sense of heritage is an important part of identity. Yet many young Muslims feel they have an inadequate grasp of their own heritage and history, against which to balance the other influences in their lives.

Role models and community communication
All young people need support and have aspirations, even if these are hidden. Those they turn to as leaders and role models can hugely influence how well these needs are provided for. Within some Muslim communities, young people often have difficulty establishing contact with religious and community leaders (local/national and usually elders) who are prepared to listen, represent their views and provide relevant guidance. With a leadership that doesn't seem to listen and offer few positive role models in the media, some young Muslims can feel lost and easily disheartened.

> • **31% of British Muslims agreed that Imams are out of touch with the views of young Muslims.**
> Source: MORI poll July 2005

Participation and engagement

Young Muslims feel that they should have a greater influence over their own affairs. Without a sense of ownership, they are less likely to make use of the opportunities made available to them. Reaching out to the most disaffected groups is a serious challenge to youth work and other services, but is critical to their success. Those responsible need to find new ways of engagement, and make projects attractive and relevant to those who would otherwise have no interest in participating. Stronger and more inclusive contacts will help to match up the opportunities provided with the needs of those who would benefit most, and avoid resources being wasted on services that have not been designed with input from potential users.

> *"Nobody has ever come to talk to us.*
> *You're the first person who talked to us about*
> *these things."*

The media and outside perception

Young Muslims are deeply concerned about the way they are understood by the public (non-Muslim and Muslim) and portrayed in the media. They feel that a lack of knowledge among the general public is giving the media a monopoly on the presentation of Muslim issues, which are often presented unfairly. Young Muslims do not feel they have much influence on the way they are portrayed and that the rare opportunities to do so are often wasted.

- **47% of Muslim students have experienced Islamophobia.**
  Source: FOSIS Survey 2005

Taking Action

Understanding what young Muslims want

Through the discussions and dialogue that took place in the project, it became clear that what binds 'young Muslims' is their potential and their eagerness to unleash it into positive action. Beyond this they all have very different life experiences, needs and abilities. 'Young Muslims' are not a homogenous group and therefore there is no universal formula for knowing how best to provide opportunities and meet needs.

However, from the ideas generated during the workshops, it emerged that their expressed needs and desired solutions can be understood as part of a wider, self-reinforcing process of *Engagement, Empowerment* and *Recognition*.

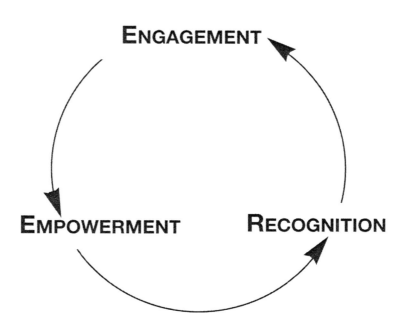

Engagement, seen both as self-awareness and as the positive and effective reaching out to others, has two aspects. It can be an active process, (e.g. making people involved and aware that their opinions are valued) or a more passive one (e.g. keeping doors of communication open so that young Muslims have somewhere to go with their needs as they emerge). It is also about being prepared to throw away preconceptions and really listening to opinions in all their diversity.

Empowerment can be seen as building on what is learnt through engagement by matching opportunities to identified needs in a way that allows young Muslims to take greater control and ownership over their own futures, and developing both confidence and ability that sustains the cycle.

Recognition is the affirmation and celebration of young Muslims' achievements, acknowledging that what they do is appreciated and encouraging them to do more.

Developing self-confidence and energy
The first step for anyone wishing to change their environment is the development of self-awareness through interaction. People need a physical and mental space that is stimulating and safe, which allows them to engage with the questions that arise as they become more self-aware.

The process is similar for all young people. For young Muslims, self-awareness is likely to mean engaging with a broader range of influences (e.g. family, education, ethnicity, friends, and religion) in their lives from which they can seek clarity in developing a coherent sense of identity.

Young Muslims look to their religious leaders, community leaders (local and national) and role models for guidance and motivation, but find it hard to connect. They need a leadership that willingly listens to young people's concerns on **their** terms, responding to their views and recognising their efforts.

"Elders miss so much by not really listening."

This has to take place on both the national level, dealing with high profile topics, as well as within local communities, getting involved and representing people's daily lives.

Simple changes of attitude and small changes in perception can go a long way to rebuilding community relationships and bypassing structural and/or hierarchical barriers, thus reconnecting young Muslims with the support networks they need.

Young Muslims are aware of what is going on around them and have their own perspectives. They do not want their opinions to be handed down to them but rather are looking for inspiration and guidance in forming their own beliefs. Community and religious leaders have the knowledge and experience to help them do this. When community and religious leaders are prepared to engage actively and honestly, this helps to empower young Muslims to build a confident, positive sense of identity and belonging.

Nazreen Ahmed and Imam Shahid Hussain - The London Central Mosque Trust & The Islamic Cultural Centre

We were both invited by the Young Muslims Speak project to attend a dialogue session with a young group of Muslims in November 2005.

The Islamic Cultural Centre has always encouraged involvement between all sectors of society and we thought this would be an ideal opportunity to hear the views and opinions of the younger generation. The programme proved to be highly successful and opened the doors for dialogue.

We believe that more awareness needs to be built on organising programmes such as these, and not enough resources are being provided. This has been a neglected area for many years. However, through these kinds of projects, more and more youngsters are now actively participating in similar dialogue sessions in the UK.

As young people are our future, it is crucial that both Government and local communities are committed to facilitating programmes and events where they can express their concerns and ambitions. Both Mosques and Muslim organisations have an equal responsibility to provide a platform for youth activities. As faith plays a major role in the lives of many Muslims within our community, it is equally important to promote Islamic youth events and seminars.

The Islamic Cultural Centre has been conducting various courses, study groups, classes, seminars and exhibitions for young Muslims for the past few years and has more plans for youth programmes this year. We believe that it is very important for the mosque to be closely connected with our youth as they are a very valuable asset for the community. We hope that through such events, it will increase our knowledge and that both the mosque and young people will benefit from an improved understanding, dialogue and good relationship.

The Centre is always open to suggestions with regards to organising and facilitating future projects especially for young people.

A strong identity is important to everyone and young Muslims identify this as of equal importance with feeling stable and confident. A strong and positive sense of identity provides a sense of security to fall back on, enabling people to engage in debate without the fear of losing key values or being manipulated.

"If you stand for nothing, you fall for anything."

Young Muslims see formal education in schools and colleges as an important provider of the information and space they require for exploring their identity. They need opportunities to learn about their heritage from an early age, so that they can balance a complex mixture of influences and challenges as they grow up.

They want to see heritage-teaching incorporated across the curriculum (e.g. languages, history, geography and culture). There are opportunities for this in 'Personal and Social Education' lessons, tutor meetings, assemblies and extra-curricular activities offering the chance for both Muslim and non-Muslim children to develop their mutual self-awareness. Here there is freedom to choose content relevant to the needs of the local community where students can be rewarded through their Record of Achievement. This is an excellent start - while incorporating heritage into the National Curriculum would be ideal, the National Curriculum is restrictive in its current form and hard to change at a local level.

Empowered with a strong, consistent sense of identity and supported by their communities and role models, more young Muslims will grow up to be confident and energised leaders of change, taking on greater responsibility for their own affairs and as role models, providing positive examples for others to follow. Recognising and affirming their achievements as a group and as individuals will lead to stronger, tighter, more communicative Muslim communities with an increasing number of young Muslims ready to make the most of the opportunities available to them.

Shazia Khadim - Learning about our heritage

Young Muslims have called for an off-the-shelf heritage package that provides the necessary information and guides for teachers to hold classes and discussions on the subject. This package should incorporate information on History (e.g. British Empire, the Mughals, The Ottoman Empire, Migration), Language, Religion (History of Islam) and Culture (traditions, role-models, festivals). Young Muslims feel passionate about having their own histories recognised and believe that this is critical to feeling confident about themselves and their identities.

The Asian Youth Alliance (AYA) has developed different workshops and activities to provide opportunities for young Asians to learn about their heritage and be able to discuss how this can impact on their sense of belonging and identity.

An example of this was a workshop on the Partition of India and the migration of many people including Muslims. This was done through showing actual film footage of the time and using this as a tool for discussion in small groups and to engage young people in learning about the topic and putting together presentations. The workshop was interactive and incorporated peer-learning; young people shared stories they had been told by their parents/grandparents, etc.

In order for young Muslims to become confident members of society, there needs to be a connection between assisting them to integrate into mainstream society and learning about their own past and cultures.

Getting involved and creating opportunities
in the community

A community with openness to the participation and commitment of young, confident and energetic members can be a powerful force.

At the same time there will always be those individuals who need more support as well as those eager to take a leadership role. The community as a whole will also have specific needs. There needs to be action on different levels, continuing relationships with those who are already engaged whilst reaching out to those who are not.

Local authorities as well as the organisations and institutions operating at community level (career services, youth and education services, youth offending teams, community mental health teams and social services) play a central role in identifying the most disaffected/disengaged groups of individuals and the needs of the community as a whole. These are the most important parts of community work, requiring the development of long-term relationships within communities and giving them a stake in their own futures and the programmes targeted at them.

Whilst many local authorities are already striving for this aim, young Muslims point out that they find it hard to get information about the opportunities and links available to them in their communities, perceiving the authorities as only being interested in their needs at the point when a crisis occurs.

Both young people and social workers recognise 'Community Liaison Officers' as having a critical role. However, recruiting those with the right kind of skills is hindered by difficulty in attracting the right kind of candidates. These should be individuals already active on the ground, who can use their knowledge to build and maintain relationships between the community and local authorities. 'Life experience' should be a qualifying criterion for these posts. Young Muslims have also explained that the demands of the 'Community Liaison Officer' role do not take into consideration the work, family and other community commitments that the most able already have. Furthermore, the method by which local authorities recruit is seen as inappropriate for the role and context, putting too much emphasis on complex procedures and forms. The approach needs to be rethought so that it is more accessible to people deemed by the community to have the right skills.

Out-reach work needs to be smart and consistent throughout the agencies involved with the issues that affect young Muslims. They have to find ways around the challenges that prevent young people from participating. Using incentives such as free travel to events, food vouchers, and crèches, not only makes it easier for people to access opportunities but also provides a sense to the most disaffected that their partic- ipation is valued and significant.

This sense can be further developed by the way organisers interact with young people and provide information. Those who want to participate are interested and eager to know how their participation can lead to actions and positive results. Timely feedback is paramount. Young people will be motivated to take the step and get involved again when made aware of the benefits their contributions have brought.

Recognising those who have emerged as community change leaders is an important part of affirming their work. This can be done through involving them and seeking their opinions as 'true' representatives of the community and/or of the young. Connecting the support local authorities provide with the requirements (e.g. financing, logistics and information) of young Muslim initiatives is important in ensuring their future success and also demonstrating that their work is valued.

There are many examples of active work already taking place amongst young Muslims, demonstrating how as both parti- cipants and leaders, young Muslims are able to bring positive change in their own lives and the community.

> ### Mobeen Butt and Shazia Khadim - Asian Youth Alliance (AYA)
>
> *AYA is a community organisation working predominantly in Croydon and its surrounding areas. It has been brought together by Mobeen Butt, a fellow of the School for Social Entrepreneurs and Shazia Khadim, an active youth and community worker committed to improving opportunities for young people.*
>
> *AYA develops and delivers ethnic-specific and culturally sensitive youth provision. It aims to provide youth provision for young Asians in Britain, in particular, helping the voice of these communities to be heard and assisting their integration into wider society.*
>
> *AYA has developed numerous projects including a supplementary educational programme for GCSE students, health and fitness courses, personal development residentials, helped with career, personal and social development and has taken part in national consultations.*
>
> *AYA runs the Asian Youth Forum, which provides a safe place where young Asian people can come and chat about issues that they want to talk about. It has also developed an online forum (www.asianyouhtalliance.co.uk/forum) which has over 200 members and has become a vital tool to harness young Asian opinion. In some cases it has become the only social interaction that some of the members are getting outside of family and school.*

Young Muslims are aware of the strong influence the media has over public perception and therefore forging links between them is critical. Muslims want the media to be a friend, not an enemy. Yet again and again, they have found themselves frustrated by the way they are portrayed and see it as unfair and unnecessary.

Huda Jawad - Working at Forward Thinking

My work with Forward Thinking has been extremely rewarding and challenging at the same time. It involves meeting with members of the different and varied Muslim communities across the UK as well as meeting officials, ministers and people interested in the issues of British Muslims and young people.

As part of my role, I try to get young people's voices and experiences heard by officials and professionals working in areas relevant to their experience. What I do involves getting ordinary Muslims at the grassroots level to talk directly to people that matter. I believe this to be a really important aspect of my work as often young people are talked about and 'represented' by adults who do not share their lifestyle, their experiences of growing up and hence some of the really complex and difficult issues that they have to struggle with. My job is about breaking that barrier for young people and getting them to speak for themselves about themselves.

The Muslim community has several paths of influence, both responsive and proactive. This is illustrated by the number of young Muslims journalists already in the media writing on Muslim issues.

There are also many more journalists looking to develop links with the Muslim community. This is an opportunity for young Muslims to engage with the local and national media and presenting their view of Muslim life by writing their own stories, comments, and inviting journalists to see what is really going on, either directly or through initiatives such as the 'Community Newswire'.

The Community Newswire opens opportunities for communities and voluntary groups to get their stories into the heart of the British media.

All this can be done through one website (www.mediatrust.org) that gives guidance on planning a media campaign and provides a direct portal to the Press Association's national news wires and both paper and broadcast media. This is a completely free service and with good planning, is an effective way to get media coverage.

Raheel Mohammed - What I do in the media

In recent years I have tried to write articles that provide a more layered view of young Muslims. Prior to the recent general elections I held a small focus group for Time Out magazine, of young Muslim women to show how they would vote and the issues that taxed them the most.

I deliberately chose Muslim women because I felt their voice was conspicuously absent despite being an intelligent, thoughtful group, and provided a welcome contrast to the usual stereotypical mainstream Muslim image - a ranting bearded man.

I have also been asked to contribute to reports being carried out by think tanks and charities. My strength lies in the fact that I can talk to both Muslim men and women living on deprived estates (this group feel that they are largely ignored), as well as being able to communicate with policy makers. The complexities of the Muslim community are rarely accurately tackled mainly because of a lack of information. As a journalist from a Muslim background I feel I have a responsibility and am capable of being more insightful in this particular area. The Muslims I have interviewed feel that they have no voice; I therefore try to provide a much needed platform to air their views without having to be filtered through preconceived ideas. I am also working with OffScreen, an art education programme, aimed at enabling young Muslims from deprived areas to express themselves in a variety of artistic ways and thereby giving them a voice that can be heard in wider society.

Leaders have a critical role here. Young Muslims are keen to see their leaders should actively initiate and contribute to dialogue on policy and the issues that affect them. Leaders have a responsibility to listen to young Muslims' views and promote them in the public arena. Instead leaders are often perceived to be placing themselves on the defensive unnecessarily when they should be pushing the agenda forward. Engaging the public interest needs to be constant and proactive, rather than merely reacting to external criticism.

> **"Local mosques need to build relationships with other organisations and not just be obsessed with themselves."**

The media also has a responsibility to throw away its preconceptions and start learning, studying the issues they report and developing greater sensitivity.

In many communities, there are already initiatives working to spread a fairer and more informed understanding of Islam and young people's needs. Such initiatives include workshops, inter-faith forums and seminars. These need to continue and aim to include a greater number of people from a wider variety of backgrounds. For example, interfaith forums currently focus on bringing faith groups together and should explore ways of including people with little interest in religion who understand the least about Islam and who often view it the most negatively.

Education can also be used to improve awareness at all levels among the public and ensure that Muslim issues are fairly understood. This can be done formally in a similar way to the 'heritage package', considered earlier. 'Religious Education' lessons already discuss values of various faiths and where education can be extended to include more cultural awareness, misunderstandings and tensions are less likely to occur. However, education and awareness can also effectively happen beyond institutions and can be further developed through more events such as festivals, and seminar series aimed at the community as a whole.

Some are already in place, like Muslim Week. However, even within the Muslim communities more is needed to publicise them.

The media has in recent years, and especially since July 7, had a knee-jerk response that it is fairly ignorant about the 1.6 million Muslims living in this country. Yet the reaction has not been a positive one. Having seen other journalists interview Muslims, the lack of empathy is conspicuous. The wrong questions are asked by the wrong people, and as a result the responses that are provided are often regurgitated statements digested from other people, newspapers and television. I doubt that there are many non-Muslim journalists that can name the five pillars of Islam, an integral part of the religion. This indicates to me a media trying to discover easy solutions to complex problems. The label itself, young Muslims, simplifies a community, strips it of any layers so that the identity can be more easily controlled. The act of interviewing seems tokenistic when journalists already seem to have formulated a conclusion and a hook to hang their story on. I have been told several times by Muslims that the interviewing process carried out by other journalists was not a positive one. Television programmes that claim to provide a unique insight into the community in fact simply produce material that lacks any depth and is the culinary equivalent of offering chicken tikka masala, a sanitised product to suit the white, British audience's palate. There certainly need to be more Muslim journalists employed in the mainstream media but there also needs to be more empathy. The media, when it concerns sensitive issues especially in the current climate, should be more proactive and build relationships with the community and not just with 'community leaders'.

Raheel Mohammed

If young Muslims are given fair and balanced representation, if the challenges facing them are understood and their achievements celebrated, then young Muslims will feel able to fulfil their potential. Those already part of the process will feel valued and further empowered whilst those at the beginning of their journey will see something to strive for, recognising the possibility of change.

> *Nobody can say Muslims don't have a voice in the mainstream media. They do. The problem is that all too often that voice is only called on to comment on issues explicitly relating to Muslims. Young Muslims have opinions on everything – from public transport to school dinners, domestic violence to Big Brother. I want to hear, see, and read those opinions and many other journalists do too. I work at BBC Radio 5 Live where producers are genuinely trying to shun the old contacts files stuffed full of convenient phone numbers of white men, and get a range of voices on air reflecting the true diversity of our society. But for that to happen, solid relationships need to be forged. A member of staff at 5 Live has now been taken off-rota in order to spend an extended period developing contacts within Muslim communities in Bradford. This will help but more initiatives are needed. And it's a two-way process. Be proactive. If a journalist gets it wrong, e-mail or write to them with some measured and constructive criticism. You'd be surprised at the number ready to learn. Don't just rely on leaders to promote your opinions and views. Push them forward yourself. Most importantly, **make yourselves accessible**. This report states Muslims, "**want the media to be a friend not an enemy**." Remember that on the other side of the fence, there are more journalists than you might think who are striving for exactly the same thing.*
>
> **Chris Jameson**

CONCLUDING THOUGHTS

Those who participated in the project are determined to see coherent and effective action taking place. There have been many opportunities to discuss, analyse and review. Now is the time to 'do', recognising the diversity characterising 'young Muslims'.

Throughout the time spent together everyone has been keen to develop solutions; some new, others building on ongoing work. All can be seen as part of an 'Engagement, Empowerment, and Recognition' process. It is clear from the examples that young Muslims offer both challenges and solutions.

This is a dynamic process involving individuals, communities and the wider society in a continuous dialogue. It is a systemic process that impacts across socio, economic, cultural and political spheres. It is the process with the potential to move through different levels from the individual to the society, accelerating and including an ever greater number of both Muslim and non-Muslim people.

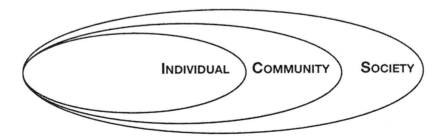

	Individual	Community	Society
Engage	• Family – ability to communicate with parents and relatives. • School – type of schooling and interaction with other people. • Role models – observing role model.	• Building long term relationships. • Identification of those who need to be approached and how they can be incentivised. • Consultation and feedback on follow ups.	• Use press complaints commission. • Leaders to lead dialogue on key issues.
Empower	• Learning about own heritage. • Learning about Islam. • Support from leaders, elders, role models etc. • Availability of opportunities.	• Listen to/give voice. • Identify real needs and provide opportunities. • Participation. • How can communities look at Islam differently? • Change hierarchical pressures.	• Raising awareness and exchanges – lectures, dialogue, interfaith meetings, 'human libraries' • Greater opportunities for Muslims.
Recognise	• Heard and acknowledged by leaders. • Fair portrayal from the media.	• Interaction with 'true' role models. • Balanced view of Muslim communities reported on the media.	• Recognition of diversity of Muslims. • Balanced view of Muslims ad Islam reported on media. • Celebration of Islam e.g. Muslim Week, Muslim religious festivals, broadcast of Imams on such occasions.

THE 'YOUNG MUSLIMS SPEAK' PROJECT

Process and facilitation
The 'Young Muslims Speak' project ran over two workshops, inviting young participants from all over the UK. Peace Direct invited people with different origins and backgrounds. Overall we engaged around 50 people who contributed in different ways and whose origins lay in 9 different regions of the world.

The first event was used to highlight the most important issues. Between the first and second meeting, participants were invited to hold dialogue session with other young people in their own communities discussing the issues raised during the first day. The second workshop focused on developing an action plan for change together with representatives of local social services. The workshops were facilitated by Muslim international peacebuilders; Dekha Ibrahim Abdi from Kenya and Mohammad Shbyta from Palestine. Their experiences and skills added fresh and clear perspectives to the British context and enabled participants to challenge their preconceptions.

Tools for dialogue
Dekha and Mohammad used a variety of tools employed in Kenya and Palestine to stimulate and encourage participants to think about their situation and the opportunities provided.

The *Johari Window* shown overleaf graphically illustrates the different ways in which we can be understood. It describes how our actions do not always align with our intentions as we may not be fully aware of ourselves, and how we are interpreted by others depends on their understanding and expectations. This can lead to misunderstandings and conflict. The Johari Window demonstrates how by revealing more of ourselves and asking for feedback helps us and others to match actions and intentions, avoiding misunderstandings.

The Johari Window

	Known to self	Not known to self
Known to other	Open	Blind
Not known to others	Hidden	Unknown

Nafs can be used to explain the way people react to conflict and how this has the potential to escalate into violence. When faced with a threat, people tend to attribute blame and all that is bad to the 'other' whilst attributing all that is good to themselves and their allies. This creates a gap of understanding that makes it easier to make further negative attributions. The concept of *nafs* provides an explanation for this cycle by explaining the life states through which conflict/peace develops from a Muslim perspective.

Relationship mapping was used where participants were invited to choose a key theme that was drawn in the centre of a diagram. Around these key themes, participants marked down all the factors that influence and are influenced by them. Different lines were then drawn between issues and factors to note the relationships between them both as they are now and how participants would like them to be in the future. This exercise helps to identify issues, factors, the relationship between them and highlights some of the ways in which the situation can be improved.

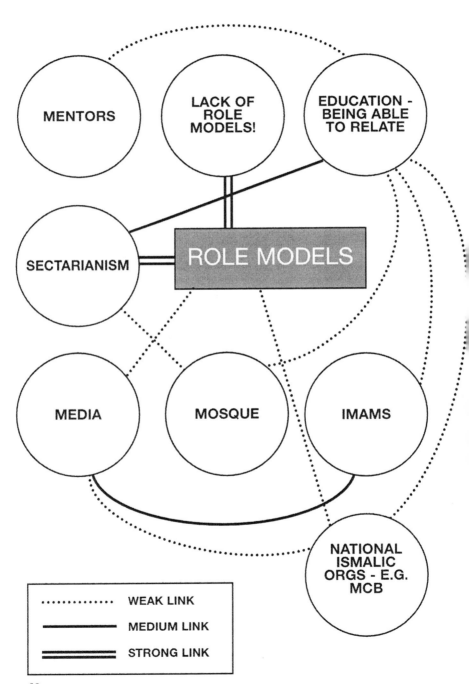

RESOURCES

Below are a handful of contacts which could be of interest to young people. There are many more, however we chose to list those that were recommended to us.

Asian Youth Alliance Forum
www.asianyouthalliance.co.uk/forum - An online where young Asians can come to chat, chill and debate about issues which affect them.

Muslim Youth Helpline
www.myh.org.uk - The Muslim Youth Helpline is a confidential helpline for young Muslims. All helpline workers are young people trained to help young people whatever problem or difficulty they face.

The Islamic Society of Britain
www.isb.org.uk - was set up to provide a vehicle for committed British Muslims to combine their knowledge, skills and efforts for the benefit of one another and British society as a whole, through the promotion of Islam and Islamic values. ISB brings together the youth, men and women from all social and ethnic backgrounds, and different schools of thought, for the benefit of all.

World Assembly of Muslim Youth
www.wamy.co.uk - The World Assembly of Muslim Youth is an independent international organisation and an Islamic forum that supports the work of Muslim organisations and needy communities the world over.

The Site
www.youthnet.org.uk - Aims to be the first place all young adults turn to when they need support and guidance through life.

FUNDING
Al Fayed Charitable Foundation
Tel: 020 72256673 - Amounts awarded: Average grant £9000. Applications in writing, to the correspondent.

Awards for All
www.awardsforall.org.uk - Amounts awarded: £500 - £5,000.

Big Lottery Fund
www.thebiglotteryfund.org – The Big Lottery Fund's Board has agreed to allocate a further £100m to the extension of the Young People's Fund Programme in England.

Camelot Foundation
www.camelotfoundation.org.uk

Charities Aid Foundation Ethnic Minority Fund
www.charitynet.org - Amounts awarded: Up to £4,000.

Comic Relief
www.comicrelief.org.uk - Amounts awarded: Up to £25,000 per year for up to 3 years.

Ethnic Minority Grants Scheme
Tel: 01383 620780 - Amounts awarded: Up to £25,000 per year for up to two years.

Faith Communities Capacity Building Fund
www.cdf.org.uk

Hilden Charitable Trust
Tel: 020 76031525 - Amounts awarded: £1,000 - £15,000.

Home Office Active Community Unit
public_enquiry.acu@homeoffice.gsi.gov.uk

Lloyds TSB Foundation
www.lloydstsbfoundations.org.uk - Amounts awarded: Varies.

Prince's Trust
www.princes-trust.org.uk - A UK charity that helps young people overcome barriers and get their lives working. Through practical support including training, mentoring and financial assistance, they help 14-30 year olds realise their potential and transform their lives.

Sir Halley Stewart Trust
www.sirhalleystewart.org - The Trust aims to promote and assist innovative research activities or pioneering developments with a view to making such work self-supporting. It emphasises prevention rather than alleviation of human suffering.

The Big Boost
www.thebigboost.org.uk – For ideas that benefit the community It awards grants between £500 to £5000, with an average of £2,500. The awards are given to individuals between 16-25 year olds or small groups (with a maximum group size of 4).

The Scarman Trust
www.thescarmantrust.org - The Scarman Trust is a national charity committed to helping citizens bring about change in their community, in the way that they want. It funds and gives practical assistance to hundreds of remarkable people with a 'can do' attitude.

UnLtd - the Foundation for Social Entrepreneurs
www.unltd.org.uk - aims to support and develop the role of social entrepreneurs as a force for positive change in the United Kingdom. It provides awards to social entrepreneurs a UK wide Fellowship of people who have received awards, research into the impact of social entrepreneurs on society and UnLtd Ventures.

INTERFAITH
The Sternberg Foundation
Tel: 020 74852538 – runs an interfaith seminar series in February 2006 aimed at specifically young people

LEADERSHIP
Changemakers
www.changemakers.org.uk - Provides a platform and process for young people to get actively involved in their communities. Its youth led learning programmes, grant schemes and volunteering initiatives stimulate enterprising minds, motivate active citizens and educate future leaders.

Common Purpose
www.commonpurpose.org.uk - Runs leadership courses. *Frontrunner* targets young people who have already shown evidence of leadership skills in civil society through their activities and aims to inspire them to continue campaigning for change in their future careers. *Navigator* is Common Purpose's leadership programme for young, high-potential individuals who are working to establish themselves in their career and are tipped as people to watch in their organisations.

Muslimaat UK

www.islamicforumeurope.com - endeavours to introduce Islam in its entirety to the youth, awakening the hearts of the Muslim women and encouraging them to realise the individual responsibility of working together under the principles of a Jama'(organisation).

The School for Social Entrepreneurs

www.sse.org.uk - Entrepreneurs exists to provide training and opportunities to enable people to use their creative and entrepreneurial abilities more fully for social benefit. We also want to recruit more innovative and capable people into voluntary and other organisations.

TRAINING
Counselling Psychotherapy Central Awarding Body

www.cpcab.co.uk – Accredited Islamic counselling course.

CSV

www.csv.org.uk/Get+Trained - provides media training for individuals and voluntary sector organizations at selected areas across the UK.

Skill Swap

www.skillswap.org - People from the local new media community volunteer to give up some of their free time to train a small group of their peers in a subject that interests them.

University of Hertfordshire

Email: counsellingservice@herts.ac.uk – Accredited Islamic counselling course.

YMCA George Williams College

www.ymca.org.uk It is part of one of the world's largest voluntary organizations and it is able to draw upon a deep reservoir of expertise in: youth work, community learning and development, lifelong learning, children's work, housing and hostel provision, health and fitness, economic regeneration.